I Am a Whale

The Life of a Humpback Whale

by Darlene R. Stille  illustrated by Todd Ouren

Special thanks to our advisers for their expertise:

Susan H. Shane, Ph.D., Biology
University of California at Santa Cruz

Susan Kesselring, M.A., Literacy Educator
Rosemount-Apple Valley-Eagan (Minnesota) School District

I Live in the Ocean

Minneapolis, Minnesota

Managing Editors: Bob Temple, Catherine Neitge
Creative Director: Terri Foley
Editors: Nadia Higgins, Patricia Stockland
Editorial Adviser: Andrea Cascardi
Designer: Todd Ouren
Page production: Picture Window Books
The illustrations in this book were prepared digitally.

Picture Window Books
5115 Excelsior Boulevard
Suite 232
Minneapolis, MN 55416
877-845-8392
www.picturewindowbooks.com

Printed in the United States of America.

Library of Congress Cataloging-in-Publication Data
I am a whale : the life of a humpback whale /
by Darlene R. Stille ; illustrated by Todd Ouren.
p. cm. — (I live in the ocean)
Includes bibliographical references (p.).
ISBN 1-4048-0600-8 (reinforced lib. bdg.)
1. Humpback whale—Juvenile literature. I. Ouren, Todd, ill.
II. Title.

QL737.C424S755 2004
599.5'25—dc22 2004000891

Watch me glide through the water. I can swim and dive like a fish. I even look like a fish, but I'm not a fish. I am a mammal.

I am a humpback whale. When I dive, I arch my back. It looks like a hump coming out of the water.

Unlike a fish, a whale can't breathe under water. It has to swim up to the surface to breathe.

Many whales make sounds, but they can't sing the way I can.

Awwrrrrrrr...EEeeeaawwweeee...

I moan and groan and roar. I make long trills and high chirps.

Scientists aren't sure why humpback males sing. The songs may be love songs to females. They might be the way the whales show each other who's boss.

Other male humpbacks sing pretty well, too. I practice and practice, so my songs will be the best! My wonderful songs can be heard for miles.

I'm also famous for my amazing moves. Check me out! I can leap right out of the water. *Crash!* I make a huge splash when I land.

When a humpback leaps out of the water, it's called breaching. When the whale smacks its tail, it's called lobtailing. Scientists think that whales send signals to each other by breaching and lobtailing.

Boom! It sounds like thunder when I smack my tail against the water.

Snort. ***Whoosh.*** I breathe in and out through two holes on the top of my head. They are my blowholes. I can open and close my blowholes just like you open and close your mouth.

Whale watchers often have trouble figuring out what kind of whale they've spotted. They look closely at the size and shape of the blow. It shows them which whale is underneath.

When I breathe out, a big mist sprays over my head. That mist is called my blow.

I take a big gulp of air. Now watch me dive. Look at my tail fins sinking into the sea.

My tail fins are called flukes. I swish them up and down. They move my big body through the water.

A humpback's flukes are unique—just like your fingerprints. No two humpbacks' flukes look exactly the same.

I'm one of the biggest creatures in the world! I am as long as a school bus. My flippers alone are four times longer than you.

The reason whales can be so big is that they don't need to carry their heavy bodies around on land. The water holds them up.

If you think I'm big, you should see my cousin, Blue. He's almost twice as big as I am. He gets the prize for being the biggest animal that's ever lived—even bigger than dinosaurs!

Look inside my huge mouth. What do you see? That's right. I don't have teeth. I have baleen instead.

The baleen works like a strainer. I take a big gulp of water full of tiny fish and krill. I close my mouth. *Squirt!* I push out the water, but my food stays trapped behind the baleen.

Baleen is a comblike structure that hangs down from a whale's upper jaw. Baleen plates are strong but flexible. They are made out of the same stuff as your fingernails. Not all whales have baleen. Some have teeth.

I have a really neat way of hunting. I dive beneath a big group of fish. Slowly, I swim in circles while breathing out of my blowhole.

As I blow, a sparkling net of bubbles makes a tube around the fish. The fish can't swim away. I lunge through the middle and swallow them. *Yum!*

Sometimes, a humpback hunts by slapping the surface of the water with its flukes. The smack stuns nearby fish and makes them easier to catch.

I can eat more than a ton of food a day, but most days I don't eat anything. I do almost all of my eating in summertime.

In summer, I live in the cold waters near Alaska. There's a lot of good food there at that time of year, so I fill up. My blubber grows thick.

The layer of fat around a whale's body is called blubber. It works like a blanket to keep the whale warm. Blubber is lighter than water, so it helps keep the whale afloat. Blubber also stores energy that the whale needs during winter when it goes for months without eating.

In winter, I swim back to Hawaii, where I was born. Everyone in my feeding group was born here. We come back to start our own families.

I meet up with my buddies. We sing our famous songs. Life in the sea sounds beautiful to me!

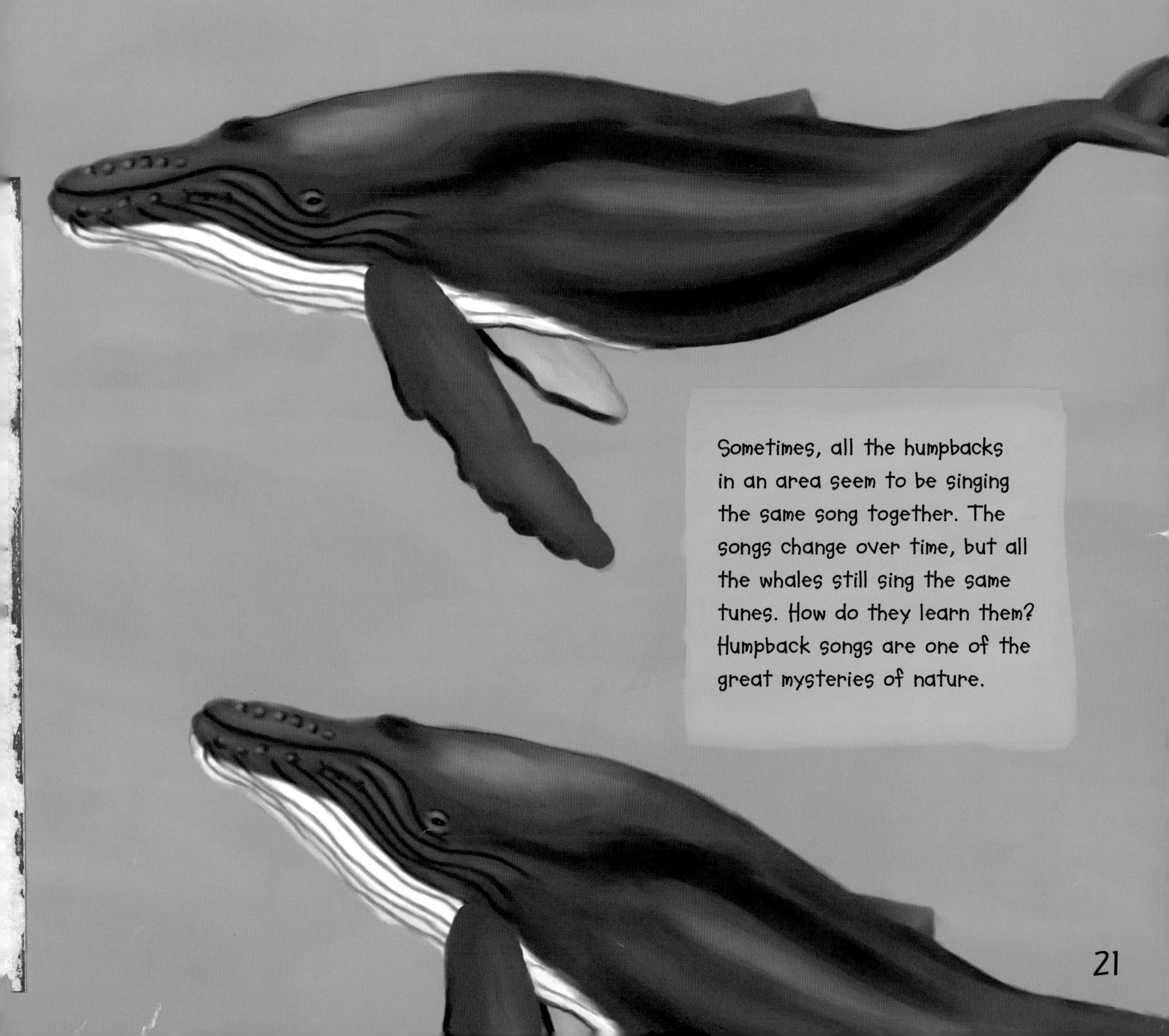

Sometimes, all the humpbacks in an area seem to be singing the same song together. The songs change over time, but all the whales still sing the same tunes. How do they learn them? Humpback songs are one of the great mysteries of nature.

Look Closely at a Humpback Whale

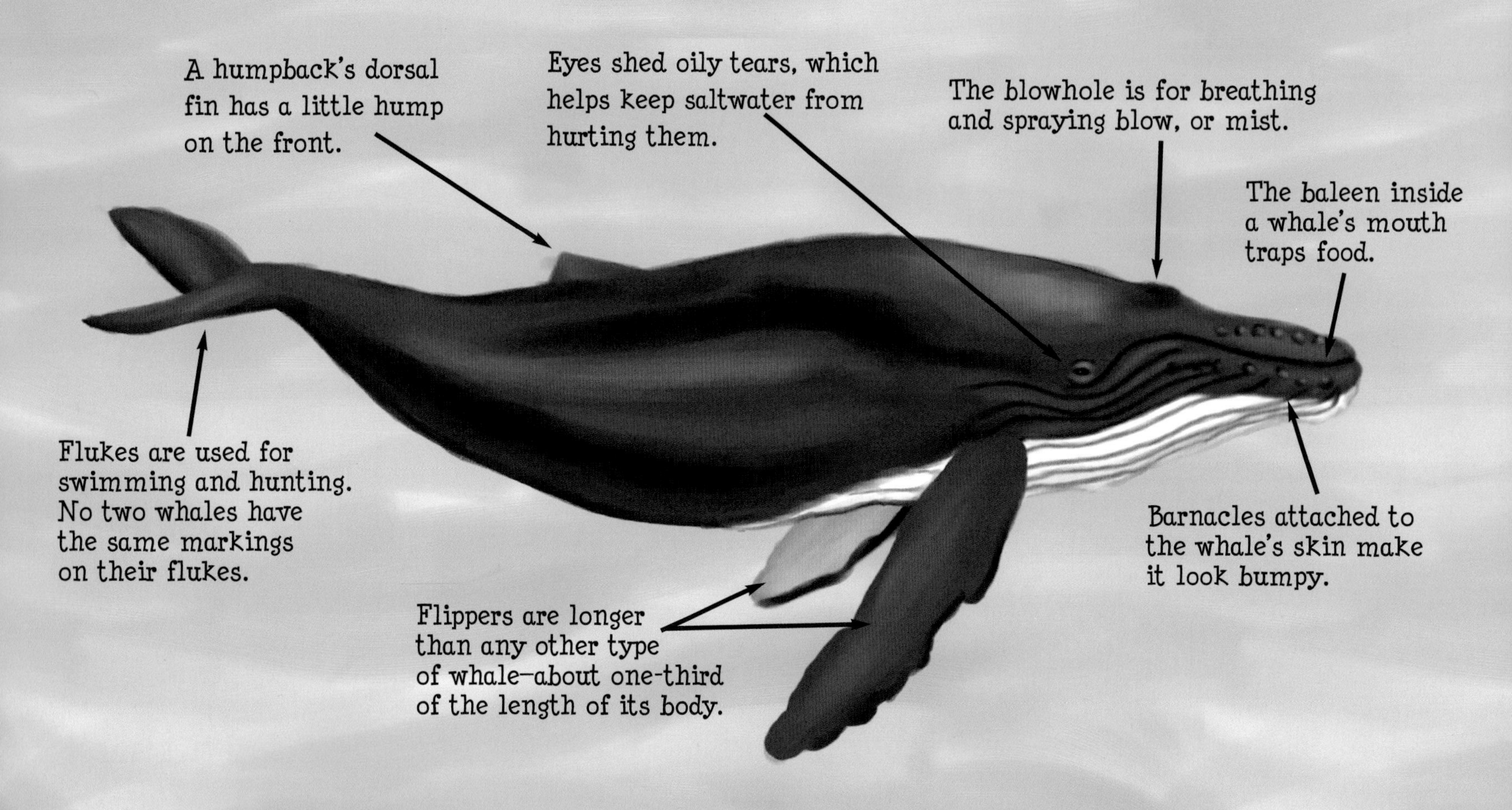

Fun Facts

Looks Itchy

Sometimes, sea animals called barnacles stick to the skin of a whale. Barnacles have a hard shell. They make the whale's skin look blotchy or bumpy.

Bad Times

Many kinds of whales are endangered. That means they could all die out. People once killed whales for their blubber. Thousands of whales died. The blubber was turned into oil to light lamps. People used the baleen, also called whalebone, to make umbrellas and other things.

Who Said That?

Whales don't have vocal cords. When whales sing, their mouths don't move. No air escapes. Scientists aren't sure how whales make sounds when they are under water.

Baby Talk

A mother humpback gives birth to only one calf, or baby whale, at a time. A newborn humpback is about 13 feet (4 meters) long and weighs 4,000 pounds (1,800 kilograms). It can swim right away. The baby drinks its mother's milk. It stays close by its mother's side for about one year.

You Go, Girl!

Unlike most mammals, female humpbacks are bigger than males. They can grow to be 45 feet long.

Stay Back!

One of the humpback's few predators is the orca, or killer whale. When a killer whale approaches, a humpback thrashes its flukes. It turns and rolls its huge body. Sometimes that scares the orca away.

Glossary

baleen—a bony plate that works like a strainer for trapping fish inside a whale's mouth

blow—a cloud of mist, or blow, that appears above a whale's head when it breathes out

blowhole—a hole on the top of a whale's head that is used for breathing; baleen whales have two blowholes

blubber—the thick layer of fat just beneath a whale's skin

breaching—when a whale leaps out of the water then falls back in with a big splash

flukes—a whale's tail

lobtailing—when a whale smacks its flukes against the surface of the water

To Learn More

At the Library

Arnold, Caroline, and Richard Hewett. *Baby Whale Rescue: The True Story of J. J.* Mahwah, N.J.: Bridgewater Books, 1999.

Berger, Melvin, and Gilda Berger. *Do Whales Have Belly Buttons? Questions and Answers about Whales and Dolphins.* New York: Scholastic Reference, 1999.

Milton, Joyce. *Whales: The Gentle Giants.* New York: Random House, 2003.

On the Web

FactHound offers a safe, fun way to find Web sites related to this book. All of the sites on FactHound have been researched by our staff.
www.facthound.com

1. Visit the FactHound home page.
2. Enter a search word related to this book, or type in this special code: 1404806008
3. Click the FETCH IT button.

Your trusty FactHound will fetch the best Web sites for you!

Index

Look for all the books in this series:

I Am a Dolphin
The Life of a Bottlenose Dolphin

I Am a Fish
The Life of a Clown Fish

I Am a Sea Turtle
The Life of a Green Sea Turtle

I Am a Seal
The Life of an Elephant Seal

I Am a Shark
The Life of a Hammerhead Shark

I Am a Whale
The Life of a Humpback Whale